Exploring the Galapagos Islands

by Dr. Michael R. Heithaus

HOUGHTON MIFFLIN HARCOURT

PHOTOGRAPHY CREDITS: COVER ©Linda Heithaus; 4 (b) ©Michael Heithaus; 5 (b) ©Linda Heithaus; 5 (t) ©Linda Heithaus; 6 (b) ©Michael Heithaus; 7 (t) ©Michael Heithaus; 8 (tr) ©Michael Heithaus; 9 (br) ©Michael Heithaus; 9 (bl) ©Michael Heithaus; 10 (tr) ©Michael Heithaus; 11 (b) ©Michael Heithaus; 12 (tl) ©Linda Heithaus; 12 (tr) ©Linda Heithaus; 13 (bl) ©Linda Heithaus; 13 (br) ©Michael Heithaus; 14 (b) ©Michael Heithaus

Printed in Mexico

ISBN: 978-0-544-07333-3

5 6 7 8 9 10 0908 21 20 19 18 17

4500661930   A B C D E F G

Contents

Vocabulary

environment

pollination

adaptation

Stretch Vocabulary

trait   extinction

cold-blooded   introduced species

Introduction

My name is Dr. Mike Heithaus and I am a biologist. I love to study animals to learn more about how they interact with their environment. I study many things—from entire ecosystems to the behavior of specific animals. Many of the animals I study are big predators. They are hard to study because there are only a few of them in a community. They also usually don't like to be near people.

I have been lucky enough to work in one famous place where the animals are not afraid of people. You can get close to fantastic species and easily view their behavior. You can learn how each one has adapted to its environment. The Galapagos Islands are so special that some people call them the Enchanted Isles. Many of the plants and animals of the Galapagos Islands are found nowhere else on Earth.

The Galapagos Islands are in the Pacific Ocean. They are a part of the South American country of Ecuador.

Galapagos Islands
(Ecuador)

Isla Marchena

PACIFIC OCEAN

Isla Fernandina

Isla Santa Cruz

Isla Isabela

Isla San Christóbal

Isla Santa Maria

Ecuador

ATLANTIC OCEAN

Ecuador

SOUTH AMERICA

PACIFIC OCEAN

Birth of Islands

The Galapagos Islands were formed by eruptions of underwater volcanoes. Lava slowly built up until the islands rose out of the oceans and grew into mountains. Most of the volcanoes are no longer active, but some still occasionally erupt.

Some plants were able to grow on the lava once it cooled. These plants arrived on the new islands when seeds floated in the ocean, got blown through the air, or stuck to the feet of birds. Each plant adapted to its environment.

Many plants reproduce through pollination. Pollination occurs when sperm from the pollen fertilize eggs inside flowers. Pollen can blow on the wind or be carried from plant to plant by insects. Once a plant is pollinated, its seeds can also be blown on the wind or moved by animals. Tortoises, for example, eat fruit and later excrete the seeds.

Some Galapagos plants can grow on bare rock.

By Land, Sea, and Air

Animals came to the Galapagos in many ways. Some of the first to arrive were probably sea lions or sea birds needing a beach to sleep on or dry land to raise their young. After enough plants were growing on the islands, other animals had enough food, shade, and shelter to survive. Sea birds flew to the islands. Small land birds and insects were blown to the islands by storms. Tortoises and iguanas probably got to the islands by holding onto trees that washed out to sea in storms.

Sea birds, such as the waved albatross, were probably some of the first animals to live on the Galapagos.

Galapagos penguins are the only wild penguins that live north of the equator.

Adapting to a New Home

Once they arrived at the Galapagos, the plants and animals adapted to their new home. They had characteristics, or traits, that helped them survive and reproduce there.

Traits that help organisms survive are called adaptations. Some adaptations are physical traits. An example of a physical adaptation is the black scales that help a lizard blend into black lava so that predators can't see it. Some adaptations involve behavior. For example, a lizard might sleep under a rock when the sun gets too hot.

On the Galapagos, adaptations were passed on to offspring and became common in populations. Individuals with traits that did not help them survive died or did not reproduce. These traits disappeared from populations. Many species that came to the Galapagos were from very different environments. They changed as they adapted to their new environment.

Land iguanas adapted to live in dry environments.

Galapagos tortoises are herbivores. They eat fruits and move seeds around the islands.

Giants of the Galapagos

When some people think of the Galapagos, they think of giant tortoises. Their shells can be as long as 1.5 meters (m), or 5 feet (ft). The tortoises can weigh more than 226 kilograms (kg), or 500 pounds (lb). They also live a long time. One tortoise lived to be at least 150 years old! Tortoises can live for months without eating or drinking.

On each island of the Galapagos, the tortoises are a bit different. Each population has adapted to the environment of its particular island. Some tortoises have a low shell and can't stick their heads very far out of them. These tortoises live on wetter islands, where the plants grow in thick forests. A high shell would get stuck! Other islands are drier. The plant life is less dense, and the fruits the tortoises eat grow higher off the ground. These tortoises have higher shells and long necks that can reach these fruits.

Forget the Trees!

Iguanas are big lizards. In most places, these reptiles like to spend time in trees. Many, many years ago, some tree-loving iguanas were blown to the Galapagos on floating tree limbs during storms. These iguanas adapted to the islands in different ways. Now both land iguanas and sea-going iguanas, called marine iguanas, live on the Galapagos. Neither kind looks much like the green iguanas that first arrived on the islands.

Land iguanas eat mostly plants. A favorite is the prickly pear cactus.

Three land iguana species live on the Galapagos. They weigh up to 13 kg (30 lb), and they spend their entire lives on the ground. They can live for 50 years. They are usually yellow, and they dig burrows. The burrows help them keep cool on hot days. Females lay their eggs in special burrows dug into the sand. They have to defend these burrows to make sure other females do not dig up the eggs.

Swimming Lizard

The other type of iguana on the Galapagos is the marine iguana. Marine iguanas are the only lizards that spend time in the ocean. You can only find them on the Galapagos.

Why would an iguana go for a swim in the cold waters that surround the Galapagos? To visit the salad bar. Marine iguanas eat algae that live in the ocean. At low tide, the level of the ocean drops, and some rocks with algae are above the water. The iguanas can walk down to the rocks to feed. However, lots of tasty algae is also under the water. To get to this algae, marine iguanas hold their breath and swim. They use their claws to hold onto rocks while they eat. Without a good hold, the waves would knock them off the rocks! If the iguanas can hold on, they can bite and swallow while they are underwater.

Most marine iguanas forage for algae when it is above water. Some can dive underwater.

A Day in the Life of a Marine Iguana

Most marine iguanas stay underwater for about 3 minutes before taking a breath. They can dive 9 m (30 ft) down! They can't stay in the water too long, though. Iguanas are cold-blooded. Their body takes on the temperature of the environment around them.

Galapagos hawks love to eat marine iguanas.

Iguanas start to get cold after they have been in the water for a while. They then climb out of the water and spend time basking in the sun to get warm.

Life can be dangerous for marine iguanas. Big birds called Galapagos hawks hunt them. To escape the hawks, the iguanas have to be able to run fast and find places to hide.

Like the populations of tortoises, the populations of marine iguanas have adapted to the environments of the islands. Populations that live where there is plenty of food grow bigger. Populations that live where food is harder to find stay smaller.

Life in and out of Water

Like marine iguanas, Galapagos penguins and sea lions live both on land and in the ocean. Sea lions spend time on the shore to rest, warm up, and reproduce. Baby sea lions are born on shore and stay on land for weeks. They drink milk from their mothers. While they are on land, they mainly sleep and play.

Sea lions feed in the ocean. They are fast and acrobatic swimmers. They usually stay underwater for less than 5 minutes, but they can easily chase down fish and squid.

All penguins except the Galapagos penguin live in the Southern Hemisphere. There are no penguins in the Arctic where polar bears live. Galapagos penguins live at the equator, and some live just north of it. These birds rest and lay their eggs on the shore. When they are in the water, they look for food such as small fish.

Sea lions have limbs that help them swim fast and sleek bodies that slip through the water.

Sea birds such as blue-footed boobies (left) and frigate birds (right) eat fish and squid in the ocean but come to the Galapagos to rest and reproduce.

Birds of the Sea

Some birds rely on both land and ocean to survive. Sea birds eat fish and squid. They come back to shore to rest and raise their chicks. Blue-footed boobies make lots of short trips to the ocean to feed. Waved albatrosses feed on fish in the ocean for months without touching land, but, every year, they come back to find a place to lay eggs.

Large and Small Beaks

Birds on the Galapagos have helped scientists learn about how animals adapt to their environment. The most famous of these birds are finches. Each finch species is adapted for the food it consumes, though all came from the original finch species that arrived on the Galapagos long ago.

Large ground finches have big beaks for crushing big seeds, but they are not good at picking up small seeds. Small ground finches have small beaks for picking up small seeds, but they can't crush big seeds. Amazingly, beak size in a population of finches can change as the environment changes. During years in which there are not many small seeds but plenty of bigger seeds, the beaks of the next generation of finches are larger. This is because birds with larger beaks survive. Those with smaller ones starve. Because baby birds inherit beaks like their parents, more birds with bigger beaks hatch.

Not every finch can eat every food. Finches with small beaks (left) are better at eating small food. Finches with big beaks (right) are better at eating big food.

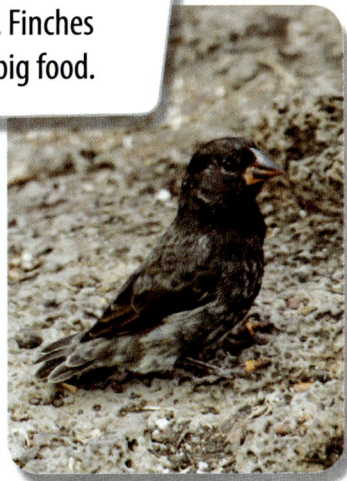

Protecting the Galapagos

In the past, many animals that lived on and near the Galapagos were threatened by extinction. Tortoises were a food source for some people. As a result, tortoises disappeared from some islands and became rare on others.

People brought outside plants and animals to the Galapagos. These introduced species, such as goats, caused populations of tortoises, iguanas, and other native species to drop.

Today, many people are working to protect and restore the Galapagos. Introduced species are being taken off the islands. Tortoises are being raised by people and then released back into the wild. The government of Ecuador makes sure that no new unwanted species arrive. They try to make sure that not too many fish are caught. There is still work to do, but these efforts are helping protect the unique natural life of the Galapagos Islands.

Many people visit the Galapagos to see the amazing animals.

Make a Chart

Many kinds of animals make the Galapagos Islands their home. Make a chart that classifies the animals described in the text. The categories are birds, reptiles, and mammals. Be sure to classify the animals mentioned in the captions, too.

Write a Report

Choose an animal from the text. Use the Internet or other resources to find information about that animal. Write a report. Describe what the animal looks like, what it eats, and where it lives. Identify any predators and the adaptations it has for finding food, safety, or shelter. Include a photograph or illustration.

Glossary

adaptation [ad·uhp·TAY·shuhn] A trait or characteristic that helps an organism survive.

cold-blooded [kohld·BLUHD·id] Having a body temperature that changes according to the temperature of the environment.

environment [en·VY·ruhn·muhnt] All the living and nonliving things that surround and affect an organism.

extinction [ek·stingkt·SHUHN] The disappearance of a species from Earth.

introduced species [IN·truh·doosd SPEE·sheez] A plant or animal transported from its original habitat to one where it is not native.

pollination [pol·uh·NAY·shuhn] The transfer of pollen from a male plant part to a female plant part of seed plants.

trait [trayt] Something in the appearance or behavior of an organism that is determined by genes.